Looking after your
GUINEA PIGS

A Young Pet Owner's Guide
by Helen Piers

Text and illustrations copyright © Helen Piers 1993

First published in Great Britain in 1993 by
Frances Lincoln Limited, 4 Torriano Mews
Torriano Avenue, London NW5 2RZ

The author and publishers would like to thank
the children who were photographed for this book;
Caroline Ficker BVSc, MRCVS, of the Ark Veterinary Clinics, London,
the Peter Gurney Guinea Pig Sanctuary, London, and
Petsville of Kingston-upon-Thames, Surrey for their help.
Special thanks are due to Iain Bownes BVSc, MRCVS, of the Grange Veterinary Clinic,
Bermondsey, London SE1, and Nigel Norris BVSc, MRCVS, for their professional advice.

British Library Cataloguing in Publication Data
available on request

ISBN 0-7112-0763-1   hardback
ISBN 0-7112-0764-X   paperback

Printed and bound in Hong Kong

Contents

Guinea pigs as pets

A full-grown guinea pig is about 25 cm long. It is plump and has very short legs and no tail.

Guinea pigs are cheerful, good-natured little animals, and one of the easiest pets to look after. If handled gently they become very tame, and as long as they are fed correctly, and their hutch is kept clean, they rarely get ill.

Guinea pigs came originally from the grasslands of Peru and Colombia in South America, where they are still living wild today. In spite of their name, they are not related to pigs. They are a species of rodents called *cavies*. Perhaps the way they trot about, their plump bodies balanced on short legs, reminded the first people who saw them of pigs. Then, because it was wrongly thought they came from the coast of Guinea in Africa, they began to be called 'guinea pigs'.

Guinea pigs are a comfortable size to pick up and hold, and although they are shy and nervous by nature, as long as they are handled gently, they quickly learn to trust people.

Before you decide to keep guinea pigs there are a few things you should think about, to make sure you will be able to look after them really well.

Have you got a garden?
Although guinea pigs can be kept indoors they are happier if they are able to spend some time out in a run on grass in fine weather.

Will you have time to look after them?
You will need to feed them twice a day, have them out to stroke and talk to every day, and clean out the hutch regularly (see page 22).

What will they cost to keep?
It is as well to find out from your pet shop the price of a hutch and outdoor run, and work out roughly what you will spend each week on food and wood chips for the hutch floor.

Is there somebody to look after your guinea pigs when you go on holiday?

Guinea pigs can roam free in a garden, but only if it is well fenced or walled in, and safe from other animals. They will not escape by burrowing under the fence. In the wild, guinea pigs do not dig burrows. They shelter in long grass out in the open.

Guinea pigs are *rodents* (gnawing animals). Rodents' teeth go on growing throughout their lives. So you must give guinea pigs root vegetables and wood to gnaw on so that they wear down their teeth.

Which breed?

Sheltie
This is one of the long-haired breeds.

This variety of Sheltie has a crest on the top of its head, and is called a Coronet.

The different breeds of guinea pig can be recognized by their type of coat. The most common breeds are *American* (smooth, short-haired), *Abyssinian* (rough-haired, rosetted), *Angora* (long-haired), *Sheltie* (long-haired) and *Peruvian* (long-haired).

You can find guinea pigs with differently coloured coats in all the breeds – some are the same colour all over, and others a mixture of more than one colour.

A short-haired or rough-haired guinea pig is easy to keep clean. Long-haired breeds, with hair trailing along the ground, need brushing and combing every day.

A *cross-breed* (a guinea pig with a mother of one breed, and a father of another), makes just as good a pet as a pure-bred.

Abyssinian
These rough-haired guinea pigs are sometimes called 'tufted' or 'rosetted', because their hair grows in a pattern of rosettes.

American
Guinea pigs of this breed have smooth, silky coats.

One, two, or more?

One guinea pig

A guinea pig kept on its own will be lonely, because in the wild guinea pigs always live in family groups. If you *do* keep a guinea pig on its own, you will need to give it a lot of affection, and keep its hutch where it can see or hear you and your family, or it will pine and may even become ill.

A lonely guinea pig can have a rabbit as a companion when grazing outdoors, but they should be given their evening meal apart, because many vegetables which guinea pigs need are not good for rabbits. They should also be housed separately at night.

Boars (males), and *sows* (females) make equally good single pets.

Two guinea pigs or more

Two boars must never be kept in the same hutch as they are likely to fight when grown up. But *two sows* (or three, if the hutch is big enough) will not quarrel. They will be company for one another and keep each other warm in winter. It is best to buy sisters from the same litter. Strangers must be put together before they are 10 weeks old.

A boar and one or two sows will not fight, but they will mate and have babies. A guinea pig sow can have five babies in a litter and as many as four litters in a year, so it could be a problem finding good homes for them all. See page 28 for more about breeding guinea pigs.

Things you will need

A hutch

Wood chips for the
hutch floor

Hay for bedding

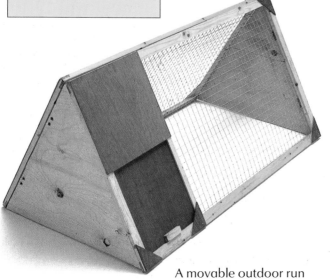

A movable outdoor run

A block or branch of
hardwood for the guinea
pigs to gnaw on prevents
their teeth from growing
too long.

Heavy earthenware food dishes are best, because they cannot be knocked over.

A drip-feed water bottle is better than a bowl, as it keeps the water clean.

Food (see checklist)

A grooming brush, comb and scissors (The comb and scissors are only for long-haired guinea pigs.)

Utensils and materials for cleaning the hutch

Vitamin drops and mineral block

Never

On the hutch floor

Never use sawdust instead of wood chips – it is too fine and dusty. It gets into the guinea pigs' eyes, and is bad for their breathing. *Never* use straw instead of hay – it can poke into and hurt the guinea pigs' eyes.

Wood for gnawing

Never give softwood – it splinters too easily. *Never* give laburnum, azalea, holly, purple thorn-apple or evergreen woods – they are poisonous. Wood from fruit trees is best. *Never* put anything made of thin plastic in the hutch, or the guinea pigs may chew it and swallow bits which they cannot digest.

A special carrying box (as shown), to take your guinea pigs home, or an ordinary cardboard box with air holes punched in it. If your journey will take more than four hours, you will need a wooden box or plastic cat basket, because the guinea pigs may wet through a box made of cardboard.

The hutch

The hutch is divided into a dark sleeping area with a solid wood door, and a larger, daytime area with a wire mesh door to let in air and light. Both doors must fasten securely.

It should be raised on legs, bricks, or a table to avoid damp and draughts, and keep the guinea pigs safe from other animals.

A rack for vegetables is not essential, but it prevents them getting trampled on and dirty. This rack has been made out of an old letter tray.

Pet shops sell guinea pig hutches, or you may find one secondhand, or build your own.

It is important that the hutch is big enough, and that it is weather-proof and safe from other animals.

One or two guinea pigs need a hutch at least 90 × 40 cm and 38 cm high. Three guinea pigs would need a hutch 15 cm longer.

To keep out rain, the roof should be covered with roofing felt, sloping towards the back, and overhanging the sides. In heavy rain a sheet of polythene hung down in front of the hutch will stop the rain driving inside. If the roof is hinged, it can be propped open in very hot weather to let in air. But *not* if any cats are around.

The best place to keep the hutch

Guinea pigs need light and air, but must not be exposed to cold, damp weather or extreme heat. So you may have to move the hutch around at different times of the year.

In winter keep the hutch indoors. Choose a light, airy place, but not in a draught or by a radiator. Guinea pigs like to be near people if possible.

You can keep the hutch in a light, airy shed, but it may need heating in freezing weather. A greenhouse lamp should provide enough heat. Old blankets thrown over the roof of the hutch will help keep the guinea pigs warm.

In summer guinea pigs enjoy being outside, but the hutch must be shaded from very hot sun, and taken indoors during storms.

Never

Never keep the hutch in a greenhouse, under a glass roof, or by a window which gets strong sun – it would be dangerously hot. *Never* in a garage – petrol fumes are harmful. *Never* let guinea pigs get too hot or cold, and *never* let the hutch get damp. *Never* use a paraffin stove for heating a shed – the fumes are harmful. *Never* keep the hutch in the same room as a television. A television gives out high-pitched sounds which *we* cannot hear but guinea pigs can, and this causes them pain.

If possible, get the hutch ready before you bring your guinea pigs home.

Cover the floor with a layer of wood chips – about 5 cm deep, and pile plenty of hay in the sleeping area. Food dishes and wood for gnawing go in the daytime area, and the water bottle and mineral block are fixed to the wire mesh door.

11

Buying guinea pigs

You can buy guinea pigs from a pet shop or a breeder, or you may see them advertised in your local paper or at the veterinary clinic.

You may be able to buy some young guinea pigs from a friend whose own guinea pigs have had babies. Being home-bred, the babies will already have been handled and played with a lot, and will probably be very tame.

There are some important things to find out about the guinea pigs you choose:

How old are they?
Between 6 and 9 weeks is the best age.

Which sex are they?
Remember, two sows can be kept together, but never two boars.

Ask if you can hold each of the guinea pigs you like best to see which you feel most comfortable with. Don't worry if they seem a little nervous. It may be the first time they have been handled by strangers.

Are they healthy guinea pigs?
A healthy guinea pig's coat should be clean and without bare patches.

Its body should be firm and smooth.

Its eyes should be bright, not cloudy and not runny.

Its nose should be clean and not runny.

What food are they used to?
For the first week you should give your guinea pigs the food they are used to. After that you can find out if they like other vegetables, but introduce these gradually.

Taking your guinea pigs home
Make your journey home as short as possible. If you go by car or train, rest the carrying box on your knees so that the guinea pigs do not get jolted about, and take care they do not get too hot.

You will want to play with your guinea pigs when you get home and show them to your friends. But they will be nervous after the journey, and it is kinder to put them straight into the hutch, give them food and water, and leave them alone and quiet to recover and get used to their new surroundings.

Handling guinea pigs

Your guinea pigs will soon become very tame if you have them out every day. You should talk to them when you hold or feed them or pass the hutch. They will get to know and recognize your voice.

When you have had your guinea pigs for a day or two they will be feeling more at home, and you can begin to handle them, and make friends with them.

It is important to be gentle and quiet when handling guinea pigs. They are nervous by nature, because in the wild they are hunted by many predators and must be cautious and always on their guard. *You* know your guinea pigs are quite safe with you, but *they* don't – not yet.

When you go to lift them out of the hutch you will find they dart about trying to escape your hands. Don't panic them by grabbing wildly. Quietly guide the one you want into a corner, then pick it up as shown opposite. Hold it firmly enough for it to feel safe, but do not squeeze it.

Falls are dangerous for guinea pigs, so practise picking up and holding them while kneeling on the ground, until you are sure you will not drop them. It is a good idea to stand the hutch on a ledge, to help prevent falls.

One of your guinea pigs may seem to take a long time to trust you. Some are shyer than others. It may protest loudly when picked up. If it does, don't think you must put it back in the hutch. Sit down quietly with it, stroke it, and offer it a treat of food. Sooner or later it will calm down, eat the food, and decide nothing terrible is going to happen to it after all.

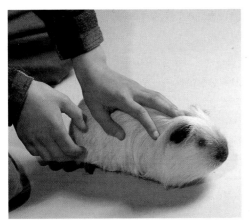

1 To pick up a guinea pig, first place one hand over its shoulders to prevent it moving away, then slide the other hand under it from the side, close behind its front legs, so that it is resting on your palm.

2 As you lift it, place the hand which was over its shoulders under its hindquarters. It is very important always to support guinea pigs' hindquarters when you lift them, because they are heavy little animals for their size.

3 When you have picked it up, turn the guinea pig so that it is sitting on your hand and resting along your arm. Keep your arm close to your body, so the guinea pig is leaning up against you. Your other hand can support it, or restrain it if it gets restless.

4 Some guinea pigs feel safer and more comfortable if they sit upright and lean against you. This is a safe way to hold them as long as you are careful to support them with your other hand to prevent them from falling.

guinea pig mix

Feeding 1

Guinea pigs eat cereals (such as wheat and oats), vegetables, grass, and hay.

Cereals
Pet shops sell guinea pig mix and guinea pig pellets, both of which contain all the cereals your guinea pigs need. If you run out, you can mix crushed oats or crumbled *wholemeal* bread with a little warm milk or water as an emergency supply.

Vegetables
A variety of both root and green vegetables should be given every day.

guinea pig pellets

carrot

beetroot

broccoli

turnip

Some vegetables for your guinea pigs

Grass

When your guinea pigs are outside they will browse on the grass, so make sure it is never sprayed with weed-killer. Grass cuttings can be given, but they must be very fresh.

Hay

Guinea pigs need hay to eat at all times. It is a valuable source of fibre.

(More about feeding on pages 18–19.)

Fruit can be given sometimes as a treat – in very small amounts only. The best fruits are apple, pear, raspberries, grapes and tomatoes.

parsley

cauliflower stalk and leaves

watercress

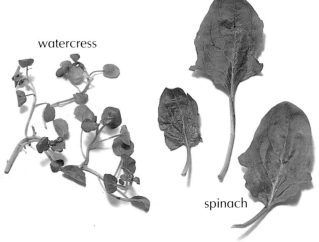

spinach

Cabbage, lettuce and Brussels sprouts can be given, but only occasionally. Do *not* give iceberg lettuce.

Some guinea pigs also like green peppers (not the seeds), cucumber, endive and celery.

17

Feeding 2

Remember

- Feed at the same time each day.
- Remove uneaten food from the day before.
- Wash vegetables and fruit well.
- Give raw, fresh vegetables – not cooked or frozen.
- A mixture of different vegetables is better than a large amount of one kind.
- Introduce any new kind of food gradually.
- Make sure your guinea pigs have fresh, dry hay and water at all times.
- Give extra vitamin C.

Vitamin C and mineral block

It is important that guinea pigs get enough vitamin C. This is in green foods and it is sometimes added to the cereal food. But give vitamin drops (from the pet shop) too, especially in the winter.

A mineral block will provide your guinea pigs with all the minerals they need. Fasten this to the wire mesh door. Do not put it on the hutch floor where it would soak up urine.

Wild plants

Do not gather these for your guinea pigs unless you are sure you can recognize the right ones – *many wild plants are poisonous.*

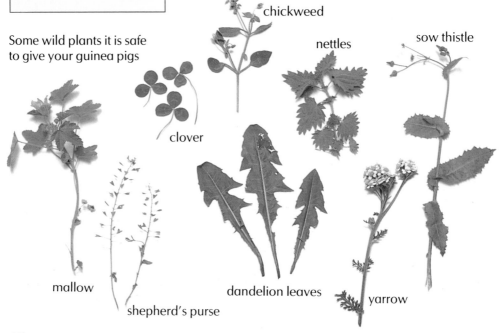

Some wild plants it is safe to give your guinea pigs

chickweed

nettles

sow thistle

clover

mallow

shepherd's purse

dandelion leaves

yarrow

18

Food needed by one guinea pig

Every morning
One small handful of cereal food.
Two handfuls of fresh dry hay.
Every evening
Two handfuls of mixed fresh vegetables.
Two handfuls of hay.

If what you give is all eaten quickly, give a bit more. You must not overfeed your guinea pigs, but make sure they have hay and a few vegetables to nibble during the night. They need to eat little, but often.

Give fresh water at all times.

Never

Never give too much fruit.
Never give wild plants which have grown beside a busy road, because of pollution.
Never let your guinea pigs eat grass from a lawn sprayed with weed-killer.

Some guinea pigs have to be shown how to drink from a drip-feed bottle. Until you are sure your new guinea pigs are taking water from the bottle, give some in a bowl as well.

19

Exercise

Remember

- Make sure your guinea pigs cannot escape out of the garden, and are safe from other animals.
- Do not put them out if it is cold or raining, or just after heavy rain.
- Shut them in the hutch at night.
- Make sure they have somewhere to shelter from hot sunshine as well as rain.
- Put drinking water within their reach.

Wild guinea pigs spend a lot of time roaming about in search of food. Your guinea pigs have all their food brought to them, but they still need the exercise they would get if they had to find it for themselves.

In warm, dry weather your guinea pigs can run free in the garden if it is well walled or fenced in. But check first that there are no gaps through which they could squeeze, and that there are no cats or dogs around, which might attack them. Guinea pigs have no way of defending themselves, except by hiding.

A safer way of giving guinea pigs exercise is to use a portable run which can be moved to different parts of the lawn as the guinea pigs mow the grass for you!

This kind of run is called an ark, because it is like an upturned boat. It has to be covered with wire mesh, and roofed at one end to give shelter from rain and hot sun.

In winter you can make an indoor run for your guinea pigs. You can use hardboard or wood, but a very large cardboard box – or several boxes cut and joined together – will do. The sides need not be high, because guinea pigs do not climb. A small box laid on its side makes a good place for the guinea pigs to run to if they are frightened by any unusual noise or movement.

Other pets
It has been known for a dog or cat to accept a guinea pig as a friend, but this is very rare, and usually only when they have grown up together. You can never really trust a cat or dog not to suddenly attack a guinea pig without warning, so they should not be left alone together unless the guinea pigs are in their hutch.

You can make an indoor run interesting by putting in things for the guinea pigs to explore.

Let your dog or cat first see your guinea pigs when they are safely in their hutch. Make a fuss of the other pet so that it is not jealous.

Cleaning the hutch

It is important to keep the hutch clean and dry if the guinea pigs are to be healthy. Guinea pigs like to be clean, and would be miserable living in a damp, dirty hutch.

Once a day
Remove uneaten food and wash dishes. Check there is enough bedding hay – the guinea pigs may have eaten it.

Once a week
After clearing out the dirty wood chips, wash the floor and *dry well* before putting down fresh wood chips.

Every other day
Clear out dirty wood chips, throw on compost heap or in dustbin, and put down fresh.

Once a month
Scrub the whole hutch out thoroughly with a teaspoon of mild disinfectant in the water. *Rinse and dry well*, in the sun if possible.

A paint scraper is useful for getting into awkward corners when you clean the hutch.

Putting newspaper under the wood chips makes cleaning easier and is more economical. But if you find your guinea pigs are chewing the paper you must not use it, because printing ink is bad for them.

Grooming

It is not essential to groom short-haired or rough-haired guinea pigs, but it is a good idea to give them a gentle brush once a week. They enjoy it, it makes them more friendly, and it gets rid of loose hairs when they are moulting.

A long-haired guinea pig needs grooming every day if possible, because its hair gets very tangled and dirty. Tangles can be teased out with a comb before brushing. Badly matted hair has to be cut away with blunt-ended scissors.

Be gentle when you groom your guinea pigs, and be careful not to poke their eyes with the brush. Guinea pigs' eyes can easily get hurt, because they protrude slightly.

Health

On the whole, guinea pigs have very good health and rarely get ill. But if they do get ill, they are not good at getting well again. So it is important to watch for the first signs of illness, *and never put off taking a sick guinea pig to the veterinary surgeon.*

On page 26 are listed some of the illnesses guinea pigs can suffer from, and a little advice about what to do. But remember, only the vet can give you the best advice.

How can you tell if a guinea pig is ill?

It will probably not eat. It will be sleepy, sit huddled up, and not move when disturbed. Its eyes may be cloudy, and its fur dull. It may drink more than usual. It may have diarrhoea.

Every day when you have your guinea pigs out, check that they are well. Make sure their eyes are clear and bright, and their fur is as glossy as usual, and without bare patches. And watch that their teeth and claws are not growing too long (see pages 25 and 27).

It is a good idea to take your guinea pigs for a check up about once a year. The vet may spot that something is going wrong and be able to treat it in time.

What do you do if a guinea pig seems ill?
Make sure it has drinking water within reach and is warm enough. Then telephone the vet's surgery at once, and explain how your guinea pig is. They will tell you if you should bring it in to the vet.

If one of your guinea pigs dies
Through no fault of yours, one of your guinea pigs may get ill, and the vet may be unable to save it. If your guinea pig does die and you have no garden in which to bury it, the vet will look after this for you.

It will be very sad for you when your guinea pig dies, even if this happens naturally from old age. The important thing is to know that you have given it the happiest life you could.

A guinea pig's claws can grow so long that they curl under, and make walking painful. It is better to let the vet clip the claws for you, because if done incorrectly it causes the animal a lot of pain.

Illnesses

Symptoms	Possible cause and what to do
The guinea pig is off its food, and makes almost no droppings	It may have *constipation,* which is most often caused by the food being too dry. Try giving more vegetables for a day or two, and make sure it has fresh water to drink. Then, if no better, **take your guinea pig to the vet.**
The droppings are soft or runny, and sour smelling	The guinea pig has *diarrhoea.* This is more serious than constipation. If otherwise well, it may only have eaten something which did not agree with it. Take away all food apart from hay and a few well-washed dandelion leaves, and give plenty of fresh water. **Telephone the vet for advice.** The guinea pig could have an infection, in which case it must have treatment at once. Prolonged diarrhoea can be fatal.
There are bare patches in the fur and the guinea pig continually scratches itself	This is usually caused by *mites.* The vet will advise treatment. The first sign of mites are tiny raised spots. The skin then becomes dry and scurfy, and the hair begins to fall out.
Runny nose and sneezing, noisy breathing	The guinea pig may have an infection similar to a cold in people, which could lead to pneumonia. Bring the hutch indoors *immediately.* Make sure the room is heated to at least 20°C. If no better in 24 hours, **take your guinea pig to the vet.**

Sore, runny or cloudy eyes	If both eyes are sore and runny, **take your guinea pig to the vet.** It may have an eye infection. If only one eye is sore, there could be a tiny bit of hay lodged in it, and it can be gently bathed with cotton wool soaked in warm water (boiled and allowed to cool). If the eye is cloudy, it could have been scratched, and must be treated or it may ulcerate. **So take your guinea pig to the vet at once.**
Overgrown claws	See page 25.
Overgrown teeth	A guinea pig's teeth go on growing all its life. It *must* have hardwood to gnaw on and wear them down, or they may grow so long it cannot eat properly. If necessary the vet will trim your guinea pig's teeth painlessly.

Wounds

Add a drop of mild antiseptic to warm water (boiled and allowed to cool), and bathe the wound gently. If it gets red and inflamed, **take your guinea pig to the vet.**

Shock

Sometimes a guinea pig dies without showing signs of illness. The cause could be *shock* – some animal trying to get into its hutch or fireworks being let off nearby. You cannot worry about every noise which might frighten your guinea pig. But closing a window and throwing a blanket over the hutch on firework night, and keeping other animals away from the hutch could save your guinea pig from severe stress.

Breeding

Before breeding guinea pigs you must make sure you can find good homes for the babies, where they will be well looked after.

Guinea pigs are one of the easier pets to breed, because the mother carries the babies safe inside her until they are fully developed. They are born with full coats of hair and eyes open, and are running about within an hour.

When should a sow have her first litter?
She *can* mate at eight weeks old, but this is not good, because the babies may not be strong. On the other hand, it is important she has her first litter *before she is 10 months old*, or she will have difficulty giving birth. The best age is five to six months. It is advisable to keep your boar and sow in separate hutches until then.

A guinea pig sow can have babies until she is three years old.

How long will she be pregnant?
About 9 to 10 weeks.

What special care will she need?
She must not be overweight when she mates, but when pregnant she will need extra food and vitamin C, and she will enjoy a little milk.

How many babies will there be?
Between two and four (sometimes five).

Should the boar be moved to another hutch?
He will not harm the babies, but if he is left with the mother she will almost certainly become pregnant again immediately.

The mother guinea pig gets very heavy just before the babies are born, so handle her as little as possible. When you do, take care to support her extra weight. Also, do not let her get too hot.

In very hot weather if the hutch is outdoors, you should hose the outside down to keep her cool.

What should you do when the babies are born?

Do *not* disturb them for the first day, or the mother may refuse to care for them. When they are a day old you can remove her while you look into the nesting space. If there are any dead babies you will have to take them away, but touch things as little as possible, and do *not* clean out the hutch for a few days.

How long must the young stay with the mother?

They should stay with her for five weeks, and must go to new homes by eight weeks old.

When they are a week or two old you should begin to look for homes for the babies – tell your friends about them, and put notices in your vet's surgery and the local paper.

When the babies are a week old, you can begin to stroke them on the back with one finger. In two weeks you can handle them gently, and put them to run about in the indoor run, or outdoors *in a run* if the weather is really warm.

Although the babies will need their mother's milk for three weeks, they already have their teeth when they are born, and after less than a week they will begin to nibble adult food.

Understanding guinea pig talk

Guinea pigs are talkative little animals. It is easy to know when they want food, for they will call – or rather whistle – to you, 'wheep-wheep!' A slower, less continuous whistle means they are protesting about something, and when they are anxious their teeth chatter, or they make a shuddering 'Brrrrr!' A cheerful 'chut-chut-chut!' means they are busy exploring, and when contented, perhaps while being stroked, they make a soft bubbling sound.

You will be able to recognize these sounds when you have had your guinea pigs a little while, and understand better what they are feeling. They will sense this and begin to trust you and look forward to your company.

More about guinea pigs

Useful information

A sow is pregnant for	9–10 weeks
Number of babies in litter	2–5
Babies can leave mother at	5–8 weeks
Sows can mate at	8 weeks
Boars can mate at	10 weeks
Best age for sow to have	
her first litter	5–6 months
but NEVER later than	10 months
Life expectancy	5–7 years

Further reading

Guinea Pigs
Katrin Behrend
Barron's, New York, 1991

*The Proper Care of
Guinea Pigs*
Peter Gurney
TFH Publications, Inc., 1992

Care for your Guinea Pig
RSPCA Pet Guide
Collins, 1990

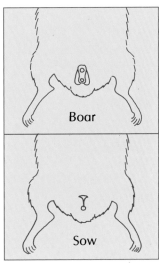

Telling a boar from a sow
Get a grown-up to help you
do this.

The guinea pig should be
held gently on its back on a
table. You will see a little
opening above the anus.
Press *gently* on either side. If
it is a boar, the penis will
protrude as a small rounded
tip. If a sow, you will see a
Y-shaped slit.

Index